M.O.N.E.Y. MATRIX PRESENTS

PARABLES
FOR
PROFIT
VOL. 2

FACTS TELL—STORIES SELL

WOODY WOODWARD

© 2017 D.U. Publishing All Rights Reserved

Reproduction or translation of any part of this book beyond that permitted by Section 107 or 108 of the 1976 United States Copyright Act without written permission of the copyright owner is unlawful. Criminal copyright infringement is investigated by the FBI and may constitute a felony with a maximum penalty of up to five years in prison and/or a $250,000 fine. Request for permission or further information should be addressed to the Inspirational Product Division, D.U. Publishing.

>D.U. Publishing
>www.dupublishing.com

Warning—Disclaimer

The purpose of this book is to educate and inspire. This book is not intended to give advice or make promises or guarantees that anyone following the ideas, tips, suggestions, techniques or strategies will have the same results as the people listed throughout the stories contained herein. The author, publisher and distributor(s) shall have neither liability nor responsibility to anyone with respect to any loss or damage caused, or alleged to be caused, directly or indirectly by the information contained in this book.

ISBN: 978-0-9982340-4-5

M.O.N.E.Y. Matrix™ is registered trademark of Woody Woodward.

Contents

Introduction iii

This One Mindset Trick Will Pull You
Through Any Tragedy 3

This One Technique Has The Ability To
Change Your Business Forever 8

Obey This One Law And It Will Open Doors
For You Forever 12

This One Technique Can Create A Brand
New Revenue Source 16

This One Thing Can Help You Succeed
More Than Anything Else... 20

Are You Ready To Burn Your Boats To Get
What You Want? 29

Are You Living Below Your Opportunities? 35

These Three Guys Changed The World By Doing
This One Thing and You Can Too.. 39

Are Your Motives Ruining Your Business?........................... 44

What Is The One Thing That Determines
Whether You Fail or Succeed?... 48

Using This One Secret Can Solve Any Problem 55

This One Technique Will Increase Your Sales 59

Three Secrets To Building A Powerful Network 63

This Guy's Vision Changed An Industry Forever,
And So Can You 66

Four Unique Ways To Getting What You Want 70

Right Now, In Your Business,
Who Are You Listening To? 77

Do This One Thing And It Will
Change Your Outcome 80

How Important Is The Power Of Influence? 85

This Guy Sold His Life For $25,000. 89

When You Look In The Mirror
What Do You See? 93

Introduction

Stories have a way of impacting our emotions. They help us make decisions, feel inspired to take action, or to become a better person. Before the written word, stories were passed down from generation to generation as an oral history. Today stories, parables, analogies help us convey or sell our message to others.

Parables for Profit is an 18-volume series with twenty stories per book to help you move an audience, motivate your teams and to increase your sells. Each series is patterned after the acronym of our M.O.N.E.Y. Matrix™ training modules. The acronym is as follows: M–Mindset, O–Opportunity, N–Networking, E–Entrepreneurship, Y–You (how to better yourself). At the end of each story there is a Call To Action. This is designed to help you build your business or if you are a manager to help your teams increase their revenue.

Each of these stories have been turned into videos that you can access at www.GetMoneyMatrix.com.

— M.O.N.E.Y. —

SERIES

1

M.O.N.E.Y.

---| MINDSET |---

This One Mindset Trick Will Pull You Through Any Tragedy

Tom Monaghan was left defeated and broke after being swindled out of all his money in a business deal that went bad. His only option was to move into his brother's apartment. He was at a crossroads in his life and had to decide between either trying again or getting a more conservative job

MINDSET

working for someone else. Tom was not the type of person to back down from a challenge, so he convinced his brother to buy a local pizzeria named DomiNick's.

The brothers bought the pizzeria on the edge of the Eastern Michigan University campus in 1960 for $500 but assumed a debt of several thousand dollars. During their first week of business they only sold $99 worth of pizzas. After eight months of arguing about how the business should be run, his brother pulled out and got a job working at the post office, and Tom was faced with another difficult choice: Should he sell the business and get a job, or stick it out and make it work? He decided to forgo a job and instead moved into an apartment across the street from the pizzeria. Within a few months, he decided to expand when he found another pizza company struggling to stay open. Wanting to merge his two pizzerias under one name, he researched hundreds of names before taking a suggestion from a delivery boy and settling on Domino's.

---------------- MINDSET ----------------

While delivering pizzas to a dormitory, he met his future wife, Marjorie Zybach. For years, the young coupled struggled to keep their business afloat. After they had their first two daughters, the girls would sleep in cardboard boxes in the corner of the pizzeria while Margie worked late. Tom would often work till 4:00 am and then start again the next morning at 10:00 am. They put every dollar back into their struggling business. Life became even more challenging when one of the business partners he had teamed up with to expand declared bankruptcy. Tom had to assume $75,000 of his partner's debt, and this extra load almost ruined him. To dig himself out of debt, he began to aggressively pursue franchising Domino's.

By 1967, business was looking good, and he and Margie bought their first home. In 1968, a fire destroyed the Domino's office and kitchen where they prepared their pizzas, and things only got worse. His insurance only covered $13,000 of the $150,000 worth of damages. To solve his problem, he continued to franchise, but this time he sold franchises into suburban neighborhoods instead of college campuses. In 1969, he opened thirty-two new suburban stores though they only did one tenth of the sales he had projected. Worse yet, with all of the franchising and expansion, he neglected to stay on top of his finances.

Checks began to bounce, bills went unpaid. Domino's fell behind on their taxes. Tom found himself with over $1 million in debt. Stores had to be closed, and employees were laid off. He even sold some of his furniture to pay the bills and slept in his car on business trips to save money. Over 40 percent of his franchise chains were closed, and he had to convince franchisees that remained open not to sue him for breach of contract.

By September of 1977, he was able to pay off his last dollar of debt. Domino's began expanding again, reaching 200 stores by the end of 1978 and 440 in 1980. He opened his 1000th store in 1983, and by 2012, there were over 10,000 stores worldwide serving more than ten million pizzas a week.

MINDSET

Moral of the story: Don't back down, don't quit. The one trick that will help you overcome your challenges is to have a winning mindset. If an uneducated juvenile delinquent like Tom Monaghan can turn tragedy after tragedy into triumph, so can you.

Call to Action: Mindset

Today:

Identify someone in history that inspires you. Take fifteen to thirty minutes and go online and read their biography. Just Google their name with the word biography behind it (Example: Steve Jobs Biography). Research their story to find the one golden nugget that will help you have a winning mindset as you continue to build your business. If you do this activity you will find when you are against the ropes you will remember the story you read and it will give you the strength to get back up.

OPPORTUNITY

**This One Technique
Has The Ability To
Change Your Business Forever**

Success came naturally to this person in the beginning, but what happened to him later proved his greatness. By the age of eight, he was selling excess vegetables from his mother's garden. By age ten, he upgraded from carrying them in a basket to pushing them in a wheelbarrow. He

OPPORTUNITY

later increased his produce business again, and by the age of twelve, he was using a horse and cart. To further his success, he hired his siblings and neighbors. By age fifteen, he ran a full-fledged produce business supplying local grocers.

For the next twenty years it seemed like continual success. Sadly, due to a miscalculation, he lost everything he had worked so hard to build. At the same time, there was a business panic which affected the banks, and he could no longer procure a loan for his company. Even with borrowing from friends, family, and his own life insurance policy, there still was not enough to keep the company afloat for more than a few months. He even lost the home he built for his parents because he had put a lien against it to secure a loan for his business. In addition, he had legal problems. He had been arrested him twice for fraud, though he was proven innocent each time. People he had done business with for years would not give him credit to buy food for his family, and the final shred of his reputation was shattered when he had no choice but to file for bankruptcy.

OPPORTUNITY

The terms of his bankruptcy barred him from owning any part of a company, but, interestingly, this man was undeterred. Relying on creativity, he convinced his cousin and brother to start another food processing business and to hire him as manager. Through perseverance and an indomitable spirit, this man was eventually discharged from his bankruptcy and gained the respect of his creditors. Though he was not required to pay back his debts, he spent the next thirteen years doing so. He also earned and saved enough money to buy his relatives' shares in the company.

All he needed was an opportunity to take his business to the next level. Deciding he needed a clever marketing campaign, he was inspired by an advertisement for "21 styles of shoes." He thought he needed some type of catchy slogan to attract people to his products. For some reason, the number "57" seemed appropriate, and when Henry John Heinz started advertising "Heinz 57 Varieties" his business took off.

Opportunities are indefinite. As long as the sun rises every morning, there will always be opportunities.

OPPORTUNITY

The reality of opportunities is that they show up in work clothes. You have to be willing to hustle, get your hands dirty, and just start. Through all of Heinz's opportunities, none of them showed up on a silver platter with a neatly tied bow. They were only discovered as he pushed through and worked hard.

Call to Action: Opportunity

Today:

Take the next fifteen minutes and research marketing ideas from different industries. If you are sales, read the covers of magazine in the grocery check stands: What do they do to grab the consumer's attention? If you are in customer services, what do airlines, auto body shops, or hospitals do to deal with customer concerns? Look to other industries to find creative solutions to market your business. You never know where your best marketing ideas will come from. If you do this activity you may find a new way to attract more customers, which will increase your sales.

— NETWORKING —

Obey This One Law And It Will Open Doors For You Forever

The populated hallways emptied as he walked along in a state of isolated frustration. Another semester had passed, and he was no closer to his goals. He had applied many times to be accepted into the elite Animation Master's program, but to no avail. His lifelong passion was to be an

NETWORKING

animator in Hollywood. To that end, his university schedule was filled with art courses, computer rendering, and live animations; but even so, he was not officially admitted to the program that would allow him the ability to graduate as a professional animator.

Only twenty people per year were allowed into the Master's of Animation program. Undeterred, however, Doug decided to take all of the necessary courses, even though they would only be credited as general education and would not count toward his desired major. He worked late on weekdays and even came in on the weekends to work on other people's projects to better his chances for selection to this elite animation program. Other students became very fond of his enthusiasm for the work and wanted him to be on their team, though they did not know he was not accepted into the Master's program. During this time, he kept showing up and creating value for others.

Slowly, however, his classmates began to find out his secret, and, unbeknownst to him, they

NETWORKING

petitioned their professor for his admittance to the program. The professor was shocked to find out he was not in the program; after all, he had been attending the classes for three years. At first, though, the professor rejected their pleas, but because of his years of networking and building relationships with his fellow students, his professor finally conceded and accepted him into the program during his senior year. And, better yet, his professor applied all of the classes he had taken toward his major.

When graduation neared, he had the opportunity to present his work to the top design studios in the world. Due to his networking during his school years, his first internship was at EA Sports, the video game manufacturer. His life changed, however, when he got the call from Pixar Studios. A lifetime of relationship building and consistent hard work had brought him to this very moment. Was it all worth it? You tell me. When you watch Disney/Pixar's UP, you will see his name, Doug Rigby, scrolling through the end credits.

NETWORKING

It is called the Law of Reciprocity. As you help people build their business, they will help you build yours.

Call to Action: Networking

Today:

Call three people in the next fifteen minutes, and ask them how you can help build their business. People do not care how much you know until they know how much you care. Relationships are like banks: You have to make deposits before you make withdrawals. If you will do this activity you will find that people will open up their networks to you and you will find more clients.

ENTREPRENEURSHIP

This One Technique Can Create A Brand New Revenue Source

Why did the U.S. Postal Service have to wait for Federal Express to show them how to make overnight deliveries possible?

The U.S. Postal Service and UPS both worked on the challenge of making overnight deliveries a reality using established systems and theories. They

ENTREPRENEURSHIP

thought logically in terms of packages and points of location. If, for instance, you want to connect one hundred markets with one another, and if you do it all with direct point-to-point deliveries, it will take 100 x 99, or 9900, direct deliveries. They concluded that there was no way they could make it economically feasible.

Fred Smith did not think in terms of delivering packages within established systems. Instead, he perceived the essence of all delivery systems to be "movement." So, Smith wondered about the concept of movement and thought about how things are moved from one place to another. He thought about how information is moved, and how banks move money around the world. Both information systems and banks, he discovered, put all points in a network and connect them through a central hub. He decided to create a delivery system—Federal Express, now known as FedEx—that operates essentially the way information and bank clearinghouses do.

Being an entrepreneur means you need to know

ENTREPRENEURSHIP

the 3 B's: the Business Behind the Business. To solve your problems today, look to other companies to discover what they have done to solve their problems. Henry Ford is acknowledged as being the pioneer of the industrial assembly line with his "unique" ideas about conveyor belts. He got the idea from watching hogs being dismantled and sold to butchers. He noticed that they were on an overhead conveyor belt system, and one person was responsible for one part of the hog. He thought that the same idea would work for assembling cars. That is learning the Business Behind the Business. As an entrepreneur you are only limited by what you don't know. As you study other people's businesses, it will create new ideas to old problems so you can advance your business. Both Henry Ford and Fred Smith changed the future by studying the effectiveness of different industries.

ENTREPRENEURSHIP

Call to Action: Entrepreneurship

Today:

Choose a completely different industry than yours and spend fifteen minutes studying what makes it unique. What are its proprietary advantages? What can you apply from its expertise to duplicate yourself? If you do this activity you will find new solutions to your problems as well as open up a new network that will assist you in creating more revenue.

---| YOU |---

This One Thing Can Help You Succeed More Than Anything Else

Of the 28 million American entrepreneurs, 22 million are sole proprietors, meaning they have no employees. When you are working in your business you will feel many highs and lows. The only thing that can turn it around is you. Your perspective is your secret weapon to keeping focused and staying

YOU

encouraged to keep going. Pay close attention to the following poem; it has the ability to change how you see your business forever. *Note that when you get to the line in bold, the poem then reverses, but it is exactly the same words.*

My Business is Failing

By Woody Woodward

My Business is failing

And I refuse to believe that

I am in control of my future

I realize this may be a shock to you but

Happiness comes from being an Entrepreneur

Is a lie and

Working for someone else will make me happy

I am more fulfilled because

Being an employee

Is far more rewarding and exciting than

Having my own business

I believe in doing the impossible and having dreams

YOU

But this will not be the case for me anymore

Everyone eventually caves to the pressure

Experts tell me

Statistically 9 out of 10 businesses fail

I do not believe that

I have the strength to keep my business going

I believe

It is acceptable to quit and give up

No longer can it be said that

Hard work, long hours and ingenuity can save me

It is obvious that

My business has failed

It is hopeless to believe

There is a chance

This will come true unless you change your perspective and reverse it

There is a chance

It is hopeless to believe

My business has failed

YOU

It is obvious that

Hard work, long hours and ingenuity can save me

No longer can it be said that

It is acceptable to quit and give up

I believe

I have the strength to keep my business going

I do not believe that

Statistically 9 out of 10 businesses fail

Experts tell me

Everyone eventually caves to the pressure

But this will not be the case for me anymore

I believe in doing the impossible and having dreams

Having my own business

Is far more rewarding and exciting than

Being an employee

I am more fulfilled because

Working for someone else will make me happy

Is a lie and

YOU

Happiness comes from being an Entrepreneur

I realize this may be a shock to you but

I am in control of my future

And I refuse to believe that

My Business is failing

The moral of this poem is the moral of business—Perspective Determines Your Reality. No matter how bad it may seem, just turn it around and change your reality.

Call To Action: You

Today:

Take the next fifteen minutes and list fifty things you are grateful for in your business. Science has proven that those who actively practice gratitude make more money, have better health, and are happier people overall. If you do this activity you will see the brighter side of your situation, which will give you the energy to grow your business.

M.O.N.E.Y.

—————| M.O.N.E.Y. |—————

M.O.N.E.Y.

MINDSET

Are You Ready To Burn Your Boats To Get What You Want?

Thought leader, Andy Andrews, tells a compelling story of why me must 'Burn Our Boats':

There was a man who in 1519 who set sail on a final leg of a voyage that was to take him from the shores of Cuba to the Yucatan peninsula. He had in his employ 500 soldiers, 100 sailors, 16

―――――――――――| MINDSET |―――――――――――

horses on 11 ships, and they were going to take the world's richest treasure. It was a treasure of gold and silver and artifacts and jewels that had been held by the same army for 600 years. Everybody knew about this treasure because army after army had tried to take it. Conqueror after conqueror had appeared with the forces and with the will to take it but nobody had been able to do it.

This guy, his name was Hernando Cortez, he was a conqueror which to our way of thinking is a horrible thing but back then it was like a job description—you could be a doctor, you could be a baker, you could be a conqueror. There were courses in it; little kids would want to grow up wanting to be one. But anyway, Cortez was a conqueror. But he was a little bit different in his approach because he knew that time after time people had gathered armies and nobody could do it, so he knew he had to gather an army whose level of commitment was beyond that what ordinary people would consider a commitment.

So rather than just sign them up he talked to

MINDSET

them beforehand, he talked to them about what the treasure was like, and what their lives would be like when they took the treasure, and what their families and the generations of lives would be like. That they would take the treasure, and how they would take the treasure, and why they were different, and what it would be like the moment they put their hands on it. And so he laid a vision out for these people, for these men.

And then they set sail. Well, halfway through the voyage he realized he had a problem because a lot of these people who were so certain turned into whiners. Halfway across they were like, "Mr. Cortez, we're not sure we should be on this ship at this time;" it was amazing, and Cortez was worried. When they got there they just didn't walk in and fight like conquerors had done in the past. He waited there on the beach, he gathered everybody on the beach, and he made them listen to talks about what the treasure was going to be like. And he brought somebody up to talk about what their children would grow up like and how their children

MINDSET

would grow up in favor and in wealth because of what they had done. He laid that vision out for them.

And then finally the day came when they were going to march in and take the treasure. And they gathered around, and as they gathered around they grew quiet, and they were ready for the speech. They knew this would probably be the speech where Cortez would say "you go here" and "you go there," and "if the arrows start flying meet me at this coconut stump, we're outta here." But what he said was three words that changed everything. As they quieted down he leaned in and he said, "Burn the Boats." And they said, "Excuse me?" He said, '"Burn the Boats! Torch the boats!" And they burned their own boats at Cortez' directions. He said, "If we're going home, we're going home in their boats"

Well, an amazing thing happened. They fought well! For the first time it had ever been done. They took the treasure, they took it! First time in 600 years, and they took the treasure. Why? They had no choice. Take it or die. That was basically the

MINDSET

choice: Take it or die. And I am sure they considered it, "Take it or die? I guess we'll take it." And they did; boy, they took the treasure.

And see here's the thing. The question for us is, what is it in our lives that is still floating the excuses in our minds? What's keeping us from getting what we say we want? What are the boats in our hearts and our minds that we need to burn?

Metaphorically speaking, what boats do you need to burn right now to help you achieve that next level? It could be anything from bad habits, unhealthy relationships, a 9-5 job, or simply giving up something you currently enjoy for a better future tomorrow. Be calculated, strategic, and plan on the best way for you to burn your boats to help you from retreating from what you really want to achieve.

MINDSET

Call to Action: Mindset

Today:

Take the next ten minutes and identify what boats you need to burn. Create a specific plan on what you need to do after you have burned your boats. What calls do you need to make? What relationships do you need to have? What marketing strategy do you need to have in place? If you will do this activity you will be able to finally go after your treasure.

---- OPPORTUNITY ----

Are You Living Below Your Opportunities?

"There once was a man whose lifelong dream was to board a cruise ship and sail the Mediterranean Sea. He dreamed of walking the streets of Rome, Athens, and Istanbul. He saved every penny until he had enough for his passage. Since money was tight, he brought an extra suitcase filled with cans of beans, boxes of crackers, and bags of powdered

— OPPORTUNITY —

lemonade, and that is what he lived on every day. He would have loved to take part in the many activities offered on the ship—working out in the gym, playing miniature golf, and swimming in the pool. He envied those who went to movies, shows, and cultural presentations. And, oh, how he yearned for only a taste of the amazing food he saw on the ship—every meal appeared to be a feast! But the man wanted to spend so very little money that he didn't participate in any of these. He was able to see the cities he had longed to visit, but for most of the journey, he stayed in his cabin and ate only his humble food.

On the last day of the cruise, a crew member asked him which of the farewell parties he would be attending. It was then that the man learned that not only the farewell party, but almost everything on board the cruise ship—the food, the entertainment, all the activities—had been included in the price of his ticket. Too late the man realized that he had been living far beneath his privileges."

—Dieter F. Uchtdorf

OPPORTUNITY

Living below your privileges is like missing opportunities. Your business is similar to the cruise ship in this parable. There are opportunities you may not be taking advantage of. There are people in your career who are enjoying all of the benefits of success. Are you? Why not? They are using technology to spread their message, they can fill a room to give their presentations, and they build relationships and seem to network wherever they go. Why? It is because they are not living below their business privileges. They don't miss an opportunity to build the business. They use everything their business provides for them to succeed, and they do it without excuses.

Are you going to come to the end of this business cruise and realize you could have done so much more? No way! It is time to take advantage of all of the tools and techniques that are at your fingertips.

OPPORTUNITY

Call to Action: Opportunity

Today:

Take fifteen minutes and identify what "privileges/opportunities" in your business you are not taking advantage of. Plan your day to use one untapped technique to build your business. If you do this activity you will no longer be living below your privileges. Enjoy your new found success.

NETWORKING

These Three Guys Changed The World By Doing This One Thing and You Can Too

Out in the country driving through the rain in an old Model T, a farmer noticed five men standing by a Lincoln touring car that was stuck in the mud. He stopped and assisted in pulling the car out of the muck, at which point one of the men

NETWORKING

stepped forward to shake his hand, telling the farmer, "I made the car you're driving." "And I'm the man who made those tires," added another in the group. He then pointed to two of the others, saying, "Meet the man who invented the electric light—and the President of the United States." When the fifth man asked the farmer, "I guess you don't know me either?" the farmer replied, "No, but if you're the same kind of liar as these other darn fools, I wouldn't be surprised if you said you were Santa Claus."

The farmer's viewpoint was quite understandable. He had inadvertently stumbled upon a seemingly unlikely mastermind group: Henry Ford, the automobile mogul; Harvey Firestone, founder of the Firestone Tire and Rubber Company; Warren G. Harding, US President; Thomas Edison, famed scientist and inventor; and Luther Burbank, respected agriculturist. They were on their way to a campsite.

Starting in 1915, Edison, Firestone, Ford and their guests, took to the road each summer in motor camping caravans, road tripping from state to

NETWORKING

state on their way to rustic campsites. These eminent men and their best friends called themselves "The Vagabonds" and eagerly looked forward to their "gypsy" trips together each year.

The men spent their camping trips competing in impromptu tree chopping and climbing contests, allowing what Edison called "Nature's Laboratory" to inspire them to new ideas. They also enjoyed sitting around the campfire discussing their various scientific and business ventures and debating the pressing issues of the day.

These masters of industry formed a mastermind. Napoleon Hill's book, Think and Grow Rich, illustrates the power of a mastermind group. Hill was commissioned by Andrew Carnegie to interview 500 of the most influential and powerful people of the time on the subject of how they became successful in business. One of his discoveries was that all of them had belonged to some type of mastermind group.

Here is a list of ten techniques for how to conduct a mastermind group. These guidelines are

NETWORKING

not rules, they are just suggestions. You should create your own principles that work best for your industry.

- Mastermind groups typically consist of anywhere from four to eight members.
- Meetings can range from monthly, bi-weekly, or weekly meetings, depending on need.
- Meetings can be in person or virtual.
- Members should have an equal amount of time to talk about their businesses.
- Transparency is necessary. No egos should be unchecked.
- The purpose is to support each member in reaching their personal goals.
- One speaker can be the moderator. However, the moderator should switch each session.
- Each member should commit to an action.
- At the following session, the moderator should hold everyone accountable to their previous commitments.
- Each member should give and receive support.

NETWORKING

Call to Action: Networking

Today:

Take the next fifteen minutes and make a list of four to eight people you would want in your mastermind group. Call each of them and ask them to be part of this group. Review the guidelines and set your first meeting within the next thirty days. If you will do this activity you too can reach your full potential like Edison, Ford, and Firestone.

ENTREPRENEURSHIP

Are Your Motives Ruining Your Business?

An American businessman in a Mexican village was at a pier when a tiny boat with just one fisherman arrived. Inside the small boat were several large Yellow Fin Tuna. The American complimented the Mexican on the quality of his fish and asked how long it took to catch them. The Mexican replied, "only a little while." The American then asked why

ENTREPRENEURSHIP

he didn't stay out longer and catch more fish? The Mexican said he had enough to support his family's immediate needs. The American then asked what the Mexican did with the rest of his time. The fisherman said, "I sleep late, fish a little, play with my children, take a siesta with my wife, Maria, stroll into the village each evening where I play my guitar and sing and talk with my amigos. I have a full and busy life, Señor."

The American felt he had a better idea and suggested that he could really help the fisherman:

You should spend more time fishing and with the proceeds buy a bigger boat. Eventually you could buy several boats, until you would have a fleet. Instead of selling your catch to a middleman, you would be able to sell directly to the processor, eventually opening your own cannery. You would control the product, processing, and distribution. You'd need to leave this small coastal fishing village and move to Mexico City, then Los Angeles, and eventually New York, where you'd run your expanding enterprise!

ENTREPRENEURSHIP

The Mexican fisherman asked, "But Señor, how long will all this take?"

The American replied, "Fifteen to twenty years."

"But what then, Señor?"

The American laughed and said, "That's the best part. When the time is right, you would announce a public stock option, sell your company to the public, and become very rich. You would make millions."

"Millions!" he cried. "Then what Señor?"

The American continued. "Then you would retire. Move to a small coastal fishing village where you could sleep late, fish a little, play with your children, take a siesta with your wife, and stroll into the village each evening where you could play your guitar and sing and talk with your amigos."

Moral of the Story: Don't be so busy making a living that you forget to make a life.

ENTREPRENEURSHIP

Call to Action: Entrepreneurship

Today:

Take fifteen minutes to meditate and journal about how clear you are with your business. What are your motives? Are you on track? If not, what changes do you need to make? If you will do this activity you will not only have financial success, you will also have purpose which is the combination to true wealth.

YOU

What Is The One Thing That Determines Whether You Fail or Succeed?

The following poem illustrates the one thing that determines whether you fail or succeed.

I am your constant companion.

I am your greatest helper, or heaviest burden.

I will push you onward, or drag you down to failure.

YOU

I am completely at your command.

Half of the things you do, you might just as well turn over to me, and I will be able to do them quickly and correctly.

I am easily managed — you must merely be firm with me. Show me exactly how you want something done, and after a few lessons I will do it automatically.

I am the servant of all great people, and, alas, of all failures as well. Those who are failures, I have made failures.

I am not a machine, though I work with all the precision of a machine plus the intelligence of a human being.

You may run me for a profit, or turn me for ruin—it makes no difference to me.

Take me, train me, be firm with me, and I will place the world at your feet.

Be easy with me, and I will destroy you.

Who am I?

I AM HABIT

—(Anonymous)

YOU

In the book *The Power of Habit* by Charles Duhigg, he talks about the three stages of a habit. There is the Trigger (the desire), the Routine (your actions), and the Reward (the payoff). Each of us is triggered by something, and then we fall into a routine, which then gives us some type of reward. This works the same for our good and bad habits.

If you want to hijack a bad habit and turn it into a positive habit, all you have to do is change the routine. When you feel a trigger happen, instead of choosing an established routine, choose to do something different. For example, if you are making calls for your business and after one or two rejections (Trigger) you go on to social media sites or check emails (Routine) to get validation or to find acceptance from friends (Reward), then it is time to hijack your habits. This is a common habit for most of us. Sadly, we waste a lot of time on unprofitable habits instead of building our business. Instead of doing this, find a battle buddy. A battle buddy is someone in your business whom you can confide in and together you can strengthen one another.

YOU

Next time you are making calls and you get rejected (Trigger), call your battle buddy (New Routine), and encourage one another to keep making more calls and staying committed to your goals (Reward).

Call to Action: You

Today:

Take fifteen minutes and identify an individual on your team to be your battle buddy. Call them and establish your battle buddy routines. These should be short calls that burst your endurance to keep you going. If you will do this activity you will find you create successful habits that will help you stay on focus to build your business.

M.O.N.E.Y.

———————| M.O.N.E.Y. |———————

3

M.O.N.E.Y.

MINDSET

Using This One Secret Can Solve Any Problem

After studying late one night, a young college student overslept. He rushed to his statistics class, arriving late, and jotted down the two problems on the board assuming they were homework. A couple of days later he apologized for taking so long and asked his professor if he still wanted the homework. His professor told him to throw it on his

MINDSET

desk. He did so reluctantly because the desk was covered with such a heap of papers he feared his homework would be lost there forever. About six weeks later, one Sunday morning at about eight o'clock, he and his wife heard a banging on their door. It was his professor. He came in with the homework and said, "I've just written an introduction to one of your papers. Read it so I can send it out right away for publication."

He had no idea what his professor was talking about, so his professor went on to explain the two problems put on the board were "unsolvable problems." They had plagued scientists for years. They could never solve them. This freshman, George Dantzig from the University of California, solved them in a couple of days because he thought it was homework and everyone had to do it. Had George been to class on time he would have heard his professor, Jerzy Neyman, explain to the class that they were "unsolvable." Since George did not have this perspective, he went ahead and solved them. A year later, when George began to worry about a

MINDSET

thesis topic, Professor Neyman just shrugged and laughed and told him to wrap the two problems in a binder, and he would accept them as his thesis.

How many of us in our home and work environments are labeling situations, problems, or people as "unsolvable?" How you think and what you think about have the greatest impact on your success, more than any other attributes or skills. Sure, you can argue the need for education, connections, or experience, and you would be right. These things are important, but they do not guarantee success. There are many educated people who are broke and miserable. There are heirs to fortunes who have squandered what took a lifetime to build. There are people born in the right time with the right connections who can't seem to pull it together. On the other side of the scale, there are countless people with a poor education, with few connections, starting with little or no money, that have made something of themselves. What is the difference? The way they think. Your mindset is your greatest asset.

MINDSET

Call to Action: Mindset

Today:

Take the next fifteen minutes and identify one problem in your business that seems impossible to solve. Call a trusted business associated and explain your problem to them. Ask them for their perspective on how to address your challenge. If you will do this activity you may be shocked to find out that someone with a fresh perspective has the solution.

 OPPORTUNITY

This One Technique Will Increase Your Sales

Do you want to make more money, have more friends, and have better health? One word: GRATITUDE. This may seem like a simple answer, but let me share the science with you. Since the 1990s, a great deal of research has been conducted on the psychology of gratitude. The two leading researchers are Robert Emmons of the University of California and

OPPORTUNITY

psychology professor Michael McCullough of the University of Miami.

McCullough and Emmons took three groups of volunteers and randomly assigned them to focus on one of three things each week: hassles, things for which they were grateful, and ordinary life events. The first group concentrated on everything that went wrong or was irritating to them, such as "The jerk who cut me off on the highway." The second group honed in on situations they felt enhanced their lives, as in "My boyfriend is so kind and caring—I'm lucky to have him." And the third group recalled recent everyday events, as in "I went shoe shopping."

The results: The people who focused on gratitude were just flat-out happier. They saw their lives in favorable terms. They reported fewer negative physical symptoms, such as headaches or colds, and they were active in ways that were good for them. They spent almost an hour and a half more per week exercising than those who focused on hassles. Plain and simple, those who were grateful

OPPORTUNITY

had a higher quality of life.

Gratitude is like a boomerang. In one study, servers who simply wrote "thank you" on the check before handing it to their customers received, on average, 11 percent more in tips than those who didn't. Servers who wrote a message about an upcoming dinner special on the checks also received higher tips—on average 17 to 20 percent higher.

Alice M. Isen, a Cornell University professor, stated that the good feelings generated by something as simple as an expression of appreciation are due to the release of dopamine, the chemical in the brain associated with happiness. As Isen explains, dopamine is released when people are feeling good or are excited by a challenge. It activates the parts of the brain in which complex thinking and conflict resolution are thought to be headquartered.

Do you want to release dopamine in your clients', co-workers', and customers' brains? Give them a little gift. After being given a little bag of candies, doctors in a study conducted by Isen were better

OPPORTUNITY

able to process the facts of difficult medical cases and to think outside the box about what might be causing the ailment. It turns out that this way of being thanked—by receiving a small sweet—had a big payoff.

Moral of the story: At your events, have candies on the table or a little gift bag for each participant.

Call To Action: Opportunity

Today:

Take the next fifteen minutes and hand write a personal "Thank You" card to three potential clients you have met with in the last thirty days. Ask for a follow up meeting. If you do this activity you will increase your ability to generate new business.

--- NETWORKING ---

**Three Secrets
To Building A
Powerful Network**

One of the greatest partnerships in TV history was Hanna-Barbera. William Hanna met Joseph Barbera at MGM animation studios. They were co-workers there until MGM closed down its animation division. Taking this challenge in stride, Hanna networked with Barbera about how they could collaborate and

NETWORKING

open their own animation studio. Together, they developed Huckleberry Hound, Tom and Jerry, Yogi Bear, the Flintstones, Johnny Quest, the Banana Splits, and Scooby Doo—some of the best-loved cartoon television shows and full-length movies of the twentieth century.

Sometimes we have to go through a tragedy on the way to our triumph. It is always best if you do not have to travel alone. Networking gives you a built-in support group and a way to leverage other peoples' relationships for a mutual benefit. If Hanna and Barbera did not have an established network of painters, animators, film crews, and production talent, they never could have gotten their studio off the ground.

Here are the three secrets to building a powerful network:

1. Hold volunteer positions in a charity. Find a charity you are passionate about. Volunteer regularly and start to build relationships with donors and volunteers. This is a great way to stay visible and give back to organizations you believe in.

NETWORKING

2. Become a power connector. When you are known as a strong resource for referrals, people remember to turn to you for suggestions, ideas, names of other people, etc. This keeps you visible to them. Ask what other people need and help them solve their problems.

3. Follow through quickly and efficiently on referrals you receive. When people give you referrals, your actions are a reflection on them. Respect and honor that and your referrals will grow. Take time to write a thank you note for the referral.

Call to Action: Networking

Today:

Take fifteen minutes and identify which charity, outside of your faith, that you are going to actively participate in. Call them today and set up a time to sit down with them and see how you can participate. If you will do this you are on your way to expanding your network.

ENTREPRENEURSHIP

This Guy's Vision Changed An Industry Forever, And So Can You

Shots were fired, and Amadeo Giannini saw his father killed by a man over a dollar. This one experience forever changed the way Giannini felt about money. Years later, his widowed mother married Lorenzo Scatena, who was in the produce business. As Amadeo grew, he helped his stepfather

ENTREPRENEURSHIP

and worked hard, and his stepfather was so impressed with him he made Amadeo partner when he was only nineteen-years old. At the age of thirty-one, he retired from the produce business, and, being a fair-minded and honest man, Amadeo sold half the business to his employees.

Though he had enough money to permanently retire, he was still an entrepreneur at heart. He approached a few investors and, combining their money with his own, he started the Bank of Italy. In the early days of banking, loans were reserved for the rich and the credit-worthy. Giannini came up with the revolutionary idea of offering loans to hardworking immigrants who were in need of money. Although home mortgages and auto loans are a common feature in any bank today, Giannini was the first person to offer such services. On October 17th, 1904, The Bank of Italy opened its doors in San Francisco, California, with deposits of $8,780 on the first day.

After the 1906 San Francisco earthquake, most other banks closed, but Giannini rushed to his

ENTREPRENEURSHIP

bank, gathered all the money, securities, and gold, and rushed out. He managed bank transactions on the street by placing a wood plank across two barrels and using it as a counter. He granted loans to people to rebuild their lives and helped reconstruct the city after the earthquake.

Giannini was a visionary. When Joseph Strauss was in need of support to build the Golden Gate Bridge, it was Giannini who bought 20 percent of the bonds to get the project off the ground. He funded many of the early films in Hollywood. It was his investment that launched the production company United Artist. When Walt Disney was $2 million over budget for Snow White, Giannini came to the rescue. Through his vision and tenacity he was the first one to offer state-wide banking. Eventually, he consolidated all of his banks under one name, Bank of America.

As an entrepreneur you never know the long-term effect your current business can have on society or the world. Too often we are focused on paying bills, meeting orders, managing inventory,

ENTREPRENEURSHIP

and resolving customers concerns. We are usually so busy working in our business that we never work on our business. If you could create a legacy company like Giannini with Bank of America or Coco Chanel with Chanel or Fred Smith with FedEx, what would you do differently than you are doing today?

Call to Action: Entrepreneurship

Today:

Take the next ten minutes and plan your legacy business. Who would you have to network with? What strategic partners would you need to have? What would you do differently? If you do this activity you will go from running a company to building an empire.

---| YOU |---

Four Unique Ways To Getting What You Want

What is the shortest distance in helping you get what you want? How do you design your goals for maximum achievement? Darren Hardy, publisher of Success Magazine and author of The Compound Effect, has four subtle and seemingly inconsequential adjustments to goals that transform wishes and aspirations into results.

YOU

1. Don't Just Think It—INK IT

The weakest ink is stronger than the strongest mind. Unless you write down your goals, they are often lost in the shuffle and excitement of new problems, challenges, and decisions. Eliminate outside interruptions.

> "Reduce your plan to writing… The moment you complete this, you will have definitely given concrete form to the intangible desire."
>
> —Napoleon Hill

2. Suspend Reality

Pretend it is only a game; play in fantasy for a while. Let the giant that lay dormant inside you out to play. If you had every skill, resource, or ability in the world, what would you do? What would you set out to accomplish? Don't filter, qualify, or judge.

> "The same thinking that has led you to where you are is not going to lead you to where you want to go."
>
> —Albert Einstein

3. Think Big

Give yourself permission to dream big, risk big. What would you go for if you knew success was guaranteed? If you could write the script for your character's role in life—and it could be anything—what role would you write for yourself? What is your Big Hairy Audacious Goal? What is that one thing that even the thought of it makes your palms sweat a little?

> "The greater danger for most of us is not that our aim is too high and we miss it, but that it is too low and we hit it."
>
> — Michelangelo

4. Be Sure They Are YOUR Goals

Many people set goals based off what they think they "should" have, rather than what they truly want for themselves. Quit "Shoulding On Yourself." Don't let your family's, colleagues', or society's ideals or expectations dictate your ambitions. In fact, if your written goals are not from your true heart and inner ambition, your creative spirit will not work to produce them anyway. All it will do is frustrate you and give you the illusion that you are a failure and not capable. Nothing could be further from the truth.

Call to Action: You

Today:

Take fifteen minutes. and meditate on what you could achieve. Let your creative giant out. If you could do anything and you knew you would not fail, what would you do? At the end of the fifteen minutes, write down your goals and the steps you are going to take. If you will do this you will find more energy and passion to accomplish what you really want.

M.O.N.E.Y.

| M.O.N.E.Y. |

4

M.O.N.E.Y.

MINDSET

Right Now, In Your Business, Who Are You Listening To?

A group of frogs were traveling through the woods, and two of them fell into a deep pit. When the other frogs saw how deep the pit was, they told the two frogs that they were as good as dead. The two frogs ignored the comments and tried to jump up out of the pit with all their might. The other frogs kept telling them to stop, that they were as good

MINDSET

as dead. Finally, one of the frogs took heed to what the other frogs were saying and gave up. He fell down and died.

The other frog continued to jump as hard as he could. Once again, the crowd of frogs yelled at him to stop the pain and just die. He jumped even harder and finally made it out. When he got out, the other frogs said, "Did you not hear us?" The frog explained to them that he couldn't hear exactly what they were saying.

He thought they were encouraging him the entire time.

—Author Unknown

Moral of the story: Don't listen to negative people. Never take financial advice from someone who makes less money than you. Don't listen to someone about health if they weigh more than you. Never listen to anyone about relationship advice if they are not happy in their relationship. The most important voice to listen to is the one in your own heart that says, "Just keep going."

MINDSET

Call to Action: Mindset

Today:

A winning mindset is contagious. Take fifteen minutes and find someone in your business who needs a little encouragement and reach out to them via text, email, or social media and encourage them. If you will do this activity you will find you will have an advocate to help you promote your business in a time of need.

OPPORTUNITY

Do This One Thing And It Will Change Your Outcome

Orville Redenbacher was always fascinated with creating the perfect popcorn. By the age of twelve, he was growing his own corn. It became his passion, and his first business, allowing him to save for college. Not only was he the first in his family to graduate from high school, but he was accepted into

---- OPPORTUNITY ----

Purdue University in Lafayette, Indiana. Choosing agriculture as his major area of study, with plant breeding as his specialty, he graduated in 1928.

Over the next twelve years, he divided his time as a local high school teacher and farmer. Since childhood, he tried to develop a popping corn that would cook almost every kernel as he was always frustrated with the uncooked kernels at the bottom of his bowl. He believed there had to be a better way.

From 1940 to 1951, he left the academic profession and was hired by a couple of businessmen who wanted him to manage multiple farms across Indiana. While managing Princeton Farms, he would often consult with Charles Bowman, the manager professor at Purdue's Agricultural Department. Over the years the two became good friends and eventually business partners.

Their first business venture was raising seed corn for animals. With Bowman's expertise, Redenbacher could finally develop the perfect kernel. In 1959, they hired a genetics expert in an attempt to develop a superior product. In 1965,

OPPORTUNITY

the company's genetic tinkering finally paid off. They developed a product that would pop fluffier and more consistently than any other type of corn. This enhanced new breed of corn needed a new name, so taking from both Redenbacher's and Bowman's last names, they titled their new invention Red-Bow popcorn. To Redenbacher, it was hard to imagine anyone would want an inferior product after trying his gourmet popping corn.

What originally seemed like a home run with their new seed quickly turned to a strike out. Farmers who purchased seeds were not interested in paying more for gourmet seeds. No one besides Redenbacher felt the current popping corn was not good enough, and then there was the price. His was too expensive for a common product.

For the next four years, Redenbacher pitched his product across the state to no avail. In 1970, at the age of 63 and in poor health, it would appear he would give up on his lifelong vision of the perfect popping corn. As a last resort, he consulted with a marketing company in Chicago that

OPPORTUNITY

instructed him to drop the Red-Bow name and to call it "Orville Redenbacher's Gourmet Popping Corn." His hometown look was outdated to the modern culture, but it was appealing and was a symbol of trust, honesty, and old-fashioned values.

Instead of trying to sell his seeds to farmers, he decided to grow his own and take it directly to market. This one change increased his current production from 300,000 pounds in 1970 to over 5 million pounds by 1975.

Redenbacher was nearly seventy years old before he saw his lifelong vision take root and start to grow. Fortunately, he would live for twenty more years and see his childhood passion for the perfect kernel become a national and international success.

What was the "one" thing Redenbacher did that revolutionized his business? He sought professional help. He did not just listen to his own thoughts and ideas. He sought out professional advice. Sometimes you just cannot do it on your own. Often times, it takes a team to stream your dream.

OPPORTUNITY

Call to Action: Opportunity

Today:

Take fifteen minutes and identify a professional who can revolutionize your business. Reach out and contact them to see what you need to do differently to grow your business. We don't know what we don't know. If you do this activity you fill find the necessary solution to increasing your revenue.

NETWORKING

How Important Is The Power Of Influence?

Airplanes and bombs could be heard in the distance. People where running around screaming. Milena Baines was told by her older sister to board the train because she was being sent to England. There were another 668 mostly Jewish children being transported from Czechoslovakia to England in order to save their lives before the outbreak of WWII.

NETWORKING

The man who made this possible was Sir Nicholas Winton. In 1939, Winton and a friend, Martin Blake, were supposed to take a skiing vacation. Instead, Blake, who worked with refugees, told Winton, at the time a 29-year-old stockbroker, that he should visit him in Prague and help with the refugees fleeing Hitler's advancing armies.

Nicholas Winton did go to Prague, and he was deeply affected by what he saw. There was no plan to save the refugees from the looming danger of the Nazis. So Winton decided to act. It was a constant uphill battle. Everybody in Prague said there was no organization to deal with refugee children. Winton contacted multiple governments for help but only England and Sweden agreed. The British government approved him bringing children to the UK if he could find them homes and make a deposit of fifty pounds for each child.

From March to August 1939, Winton worked as a stockbroker by day and a rescue worker at night to get the kids to the UK. Winton advertised in British newspapers and in churches and temples

NETWORKING

to find families. He raised money for transportation and managed logistics—even forging entry permits when the government was moving too slowly.

Winton saved 669 children but kept the heroic deeds to himself for almost 50 years. His wife, Grete, didn't even know about his rescue efforts until 1988 when she found his scrapbook in the attic, with records, photos, names, and documents from his efforts. With his wife's encouragement, Winton shared his story, which led to his appearance on the BBC television program That's Life. What Winton did not know was that the audience was filled with the children whose lives he saved.

Years later when asked for advice by a class doing a history project, Nicholas Winton said, "Don't be content in your life just to do no wrong. Be prepared every day to try to do some good." The only reason why Winton was able to do so much good was because his friend Marin Blake was a positive influence on him. Together they networked to save children and future generations.

NETWORKING

Call to Action: Networking

Today:

Take fifteen minutes and identify someone in your business that you want to network with to make a difference. Call them and set up a time this week to volunteer or give back. If you do this activity you too, like Winton, will make a difference in the world.

ENTREPRENEURSHIP

This Guy Sold His Life For $25,000.

Wally Amos is an innovator. After graduating secretarial school, he landed a job at the William Morris Agency. Eventually, he became the agency's first African American talent agent. Amos attracted clients by sending them chocolate chip cookies along with an invitation to visit him. He represented superstars, such as Diana Ross & the Supremes and

ENTREPRENEURSHIP

Simon & Garfunkel. After a few years, he decided to turn his passion for chocolate chip cookies into a real business. He was able to secure a loan from musician Marvin Gaye, and the first Famous Amos store opened in 1975 in Los Angeles.

During its first year in business, Famous Amos had sales of $300,000, and Wally Amos's smiling face became increasingly well known since it was featured on every tin or bag of cookies. Famous Amos was selling $5 million worth of cookies by 1980, and just two years later, sales had rocketed to $12 million. Sadly, by 1985, he was losing money and his identity. Over the years, Amos had sold many shares to outside investors. When he lost a majority of the company, they not only took the company from him, they also took his identity because it was tied into the brand identity. He was banned from using his name or likeness in any future food venture.

While on tour promoting his first book, *The Famous Amos Story: The Face that Launched a Thousand Chips,* he was notified that his home

ENTREPRENEURSHIP

had been auctioned off because he was fourteen months late on his mortgage. After a couple of years Amos's cookie craving returned. He started producing high-priced hazelnut cookies under the name Wally Amos Presents. But the Famous Amos Company sued, contending trademark infringement, so he changed the name to Uncle Noname. In 1992, the Uncle Noname Cookie Company filed bankruptcy claiming $1.3 million of debt.

Fortunately, by 2000, the Keebler Company had purchased Famous Amos Cookies, which had been bought and sold four different times. They asked Amos to join them as their spokesmen for the twenty-five year anniversary of Famous Amos. As a thank you, they legally gave him his name and likeness back so that he could use it in his newest venture.

Amos had abandoned cookies and was now focusing on muffins. This gift from Keebler propelled his new muffin business by changing the name to Uncle Wally's Muffin Co. By 2007, they were producing over 250 million muffins. In 2010, they

ENTREPRENEURSHIP

made over 1 billion. His muffins are sold from Costco to Albertson's and other major retail stores.

Famous Amos lost his company and his identity because he took his eye off of his business and put it in the hands of other people. What are you doing to protect yourself?

Call to Action: Entrepreneurship

Today:

Take fifteen minutes and talk to your accountant, attorney or business strategist. Is your personal company structured properly? If you do this activity you will protect your future assets.

YOU

When You Look
In The Mirror
What Do You See?

When you get what you want in your struggle for self,
And the world makes you King for a day,
Then go to the mirror and look at yourself,
And see what that guy has to say.

For it isn't your Father, or Mother, or Wife,
Whose judgment upon you must pass.
The feller whose verdict counts most in your life

---------------------- | YOU | ----------------------

Is the guy staring back from the glass.

He's the feller to please, never mind all the rest,
For he's with you clear up to the end,
And you've passed your most dangerous, difficult test
If the guy in the glass is your friend.

You may be like Jack Horner and "chisel" a plum,
And think you're a wonderful guy,
But the man in the glass says you're only a bum
If you can't look him straight in the eye.

You can fool the whole world down the pathway of years,
And get pats on the back as you pass,
But your final reward will be heartaches and tears
If you've cheated the guy in the glass.

© *1934 The Guy In the Glass, Dale Wimbrow*

This poem was written by Dale Wimbrow in 1934 at the height of the Great Depression. Unemployment was at an all time high of 22 percent. In the heartland of America, the Midwest was suffering from a drought where some 35 million acres of farmland were utterly destroyed and a further 225 million acres were in danger. There were political challenges around the world with dictators causing mass genocide. This poem was a reflection of their times almost a a hundred years ago.

Now more than ever we need to be reminded of the power of personal responsibility. This applies to our individual lives, companies, governments, schools, and communities. It is often said, a lesson is repeated until it is learned. If we do not want to repeat our past, let us embrace this moment and make a change.

Call to Action: You

Today:

Take fifteen minutes and do a personal inventory of your character, integrity, and motives. Are you taking personal responsibility for your actions? If not, what changes do you need to make? Remember, people want to do business with others they know, like, and trust.

www.ingramcontent.com/pod-product-compliance
Lightning Source LLC
Chambersburg PA
CBHW070544300426
44113CB00011B/1791